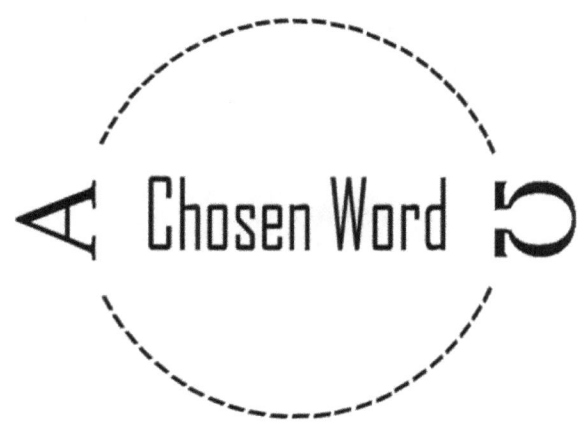

John 15:16 (NIV)
You did not choose me, but I chose you and appointed you so that you might go and bear fruit—
fruit that will last—and so that whatever you ask in my name the Father will give you.

John 1:1 (NIV)
In the beginning was the Word, and the Word was with God, and the Word was God.

Revelation 22:13 (NIV)
I am the Alpha and the Omega, the First and the Last, the Beginning and the End.

CHOSEN WORD FOR EDUCATORS AND SUPPORTERS

Tricia Delice, M.Ed., MHRM

BK Royston Publishing
Jeffersonville, IN
http://www.bkroystonpublishing.com
bkroystonpublishing@gmail.com

© Copyright 2025

All Rights Reserved. No part of this book may be reproduced, stored in a retrieval system, or transmitted by any means without the written permission of the author.

Cover Design and Photography: Tricia Delice

Logo: S. Jonah Delice

ISBN-13: 978-1-967282-46-3

King James Version Scriptural Text – Public Domain

New International Version (NIV) - Holy Bible, New International Version®, NIV® Copyright ©1973, 1978, 1984, 2011 by Biblica, Inc.® Used by permission. All rights reserved worldwide.

Printed in the United States of America

DEDICATION

This book is dedicated to my father

Samuel J. Delice, Sr.

(1943 - 1989)

He lived.

He loved.

He laughed

He left.

He lingers.

In loving memory of the greatest man that I have ever known!

Keep believing. Keep praying. Keep pushing.

TAD

ACKNOWLEDGEMENTS

I would like to start by thanking my Lord and Savior, Jesus Christ, for choosing me to share His message with the world. He spoke these words to me in John 15:16, "You did not choose me, but I chose you and appointed you so that you might go and bear fruit – fruit that will last – and so whatever you ask in my name the Father will give you".

His promise, my purpose!!

Next, a heartfelt and eternal thank you to my parents, Samuel J. Delice Sr., and Monica Delice, for their bravery and immeasurable sacrifices made to pursue a better life for our family. I am forever grateful to my South Carolina family, Monica, Dr. Sandee, Julie, Jonah, Alicia, Elvira, and Joseph, for their love and selflessness that have not wavered through every personal, professional, medical, and spiritual season of my life. Words are not sufficient to express my sincere gratitude for your genuine love and support.

I would also like to say "thank you" to my siblings, Juliette, Samuel Jr., Dr. Sandee, Julie, Jonathan, and Leon, for their love and encouragement through the years!

My gratitude would not be complete without acknowledging my Coureur and Dujon families. Thank you for opening your homes and hearts to our Delice crew on so many occasions where lifelong bonds were formed and treasured memories were made through the years.

Proverbs 16:9 reminds us, "In their hearts humans plan their course, but the Lord establishes their steps." I am grateful for the spiritual guidance and covering from my Pastors, First Ladies and circle of amazing prayer warriors, who have prayed for and with me as I surrendered my will to God and developed a closer relationship that allows me to recognize His voice and directions for my life. Thank you for filling my cup and fanning my embers to not only start a fire, but to keep it burning by serving, nurturing, leading, encouraging and praying for generations for the glory of God.

Lastly, I am blessed to love and be loved by numerous relatives and friends. Thank you ALL for increasing my love, joy, peace, and happiness along this beautiful journey called life!

I pray this devotional changes lives, renews faith, restores hope, and creates new stories that define love and purpose for the glory of God!

You are CHOSEN!

Tricia A. Delice

Recommended Use

The design.
This devotional was originally designed to encourage educators based on an academic calendar year. As the words poured onto the pages, it became evident that they were just as applicable to supporters as educators. This can be used by anyone seeking a daily word but also has the need for a daily, weekly, or monthly calendar.

The layout.
For many educational institutions, the average school year is 180 days or 36 weeks. The devotional has 36 weekly devotions, verses, and prayers.

The recommendation.
The recommendation is to reread the devotion and prayer each day for a minimum of five days. As you pray and reflect, ask God to show you what He needs you to do each week. Reflect on how God speaks to you initially, and subsequently, if there are any changes or revelations by the end of the week.

The sequence.
First: The blank monthly calendar
This devotional was designed to start at any time. The calendars are blank and should be filled in with the month and dates based on personal start dates.

Second: The weekly devotion
Each week has one devotion, verse, and prayer. The weekly devotions are accompanied by a journal and reflection page to record how God is speaking to, through, and around you throughout the week.

Third: The daily/weekly planner
The daily/weekly planner provides a snapshot of your week. It is designed to help keep you on track at a glance while managing daily/weekly tasks more efficiently. This can be used to track a variety of "to do" items such as: meals, fitness, meetings, conferences, medical appointments, church or community gatherings, hobbies, social clubs etc.

Most Importantly.
Chosen Word for Educators and Supporters is yours - do what works best for you!!
Please share how you're using it on Instagram @ chosenword1516 or via email at chosenword1516@gmail.com.

God bless and enjoy!!
You are chosen!

TABLE OF CONTENTS

Dedication	iii
Acknowledgements	iv
Recommended Use	v
Week 1 - Set the Tone	3
Week 2 - The Practice of Pausing	7
Week 3 - Chosen	11
Week 4 - Priorities	15
Week 5 - Kingdom Kids	21
Week 6 - Overcomer	25
Week 7 - Release and Lean	29
Week 8 - Rest in the Shadows	33
Week 9 - Woe to Worship	39
Week 10 - I am CHOSEN	43
Week 11 - God is Faithful	47
Week 12 - A Heart to Serve	51
Week 13 - God's Masterpiece	57
Week 14 - Transform and Renew	61
Week 15 - Surrender	65
Week 16 - A Fixed Gaze	69
Week 17 - Committed to My Assignment	75
Week 18 - Everyone Stumbles	79
Week 19 - Choosing Humility	83
Week 20 - The Ultimate Counselor	87
Week 21 - Guaranteed Promises	93
Week 22 - Early in the Morning	97
Week 23 - Fruit Bearers	101
Week 24 - Be a Beacon	105

Week 25 - Generous Wisdom	111
Week 26 - God's Hands	115
Week 27 - All is Well	119
Week 28 - Devoted Prayers	123
Week 29 - Darkness to Light	129
Week 30 - Your Grace is Sufficient	133
Week 31 - Do Not Be Anxious	137
Week 32 - Rest For the Weary	141
Week 33 - Healing Waters	147
Week 34 - Feed My Sheep	151
Week 35 - Lacking Nothing	155
Week 36 - The Greatest Commandments	159

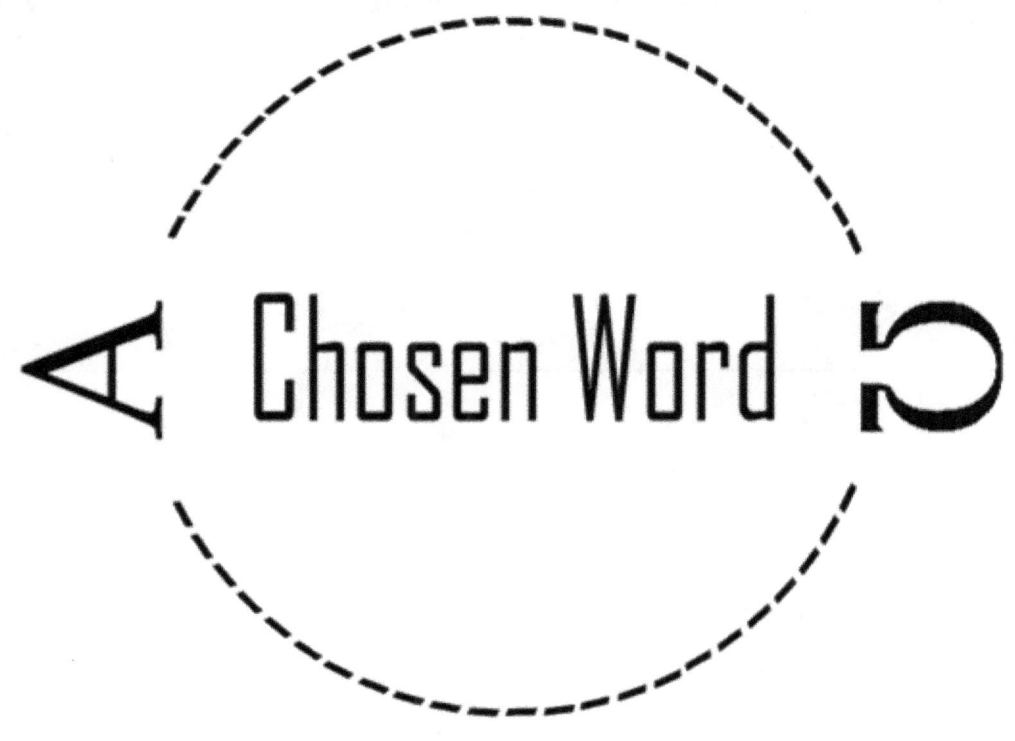

CHOSEN WORD FOR EDUCATORS AND SUPPORTERS

Month of_____

SUNDAY	MONDAY	TUESDAY	WEDNESDAY

THURSDAY	FRIDAY	SATURDAY	NOTES

Week 1

Set the Tone

At the start of every day, we have a new opportunity to set the tone for our day. God gives us the strength, with the help of the Holy Spirit, to shift the atmosphere when we enter different environments. In any given situation, we can choose to respond to negativity with love or we can add fuel to the flame.

Jesus provided the model prayer to His disciples as a guide for prayer. God isn't concerned with having a vibrant vocabulary or knowing the right things to say. What He desires is an honest and authentic heart that comes to Him like a child, expressing desires and seeking an earnest and loving response from our Heavenly Father.

As we approach God's throne of grace each day, let us be intentional about being honest with Him and waiting patiently for His answers to our prayers. God hears our prayers. If we believe that God answers prayers with a "yes", we must also believe when He answers with "not yet" or "no". As we devote our time to building a relationship with God over the course of 36 weeks, let us be content, but not complacent. We will approach God with a heart of gratitude for what we currently have but also in expectation of all the great things He still has in store for us.

Prayer:

Dear Lord,
My Father in Heaven, holy is Your name. I believe Your will is accomplished on earth as it is done in Heaven. Please give me what I need for today. Forgive me for my sins, but also give me a heart that forgives others. Do not allow me to be tempted by the things that are not pleasing in Your sight. Thank You for protecting and blessing me, my family, friends, students, administrators, coworkers, and leaders. Help me to do my best not only as a servant in Your kingdom, but as a child of the King. I receive Your power through the Holy Spirit to live a life that glorifies You as I am led by You and also lead others. Grant me peace, purpose, and prosperity in Your kingdom. Forever and ever,

In Jesus' name, Amen!

Scripture: Matthew 6:9-13 (KJV)

After this manner therefore pray ye: Our Father which art in heaven, Hallowed be thy name. Thy kingdom come, Thy will be done in earth, as it is in Heaven. Give us this day our daily bread. And forgive us our debts, as we forgive our debtors. And lead us not into temptation, but deliver us from evil: For thine is the kingdom, and the power, and the glory, forever. Amen.

Reflection and Prayer

Week of _____

Sunday:

_____

_____

Monday:

_____

_____

Tuesday:

_____

_____

Wednesday:

_____

_____

Thursday:

_____

_____

Friday:

_____

_____

Saturday:

_____

_____

	Sunday	Monday	Tuesday
3:00 - 4:00			
4:00 - 5:00			
5:00 - 6:00			
6:00 - 7:00			
7:00 - 8:00			
8:00 - 9:00			
9:00 - 10:00			
10:00 - 11:00			
11:00 - 12:00			
12:00 - 1:00			
1:00 - 2:00			
2:00 - 3:00			
3:00 - 4:00			
4:00 - 5:00			
5:00 - 6:00			
6:00 - 7:00			
7:00 - 8:00			

Wednesday	Thursday	Friday	Saturday

Week 2
The Practice of Pausing

Recall a time when something was said that needed an immediate response. The words felt like a ball of fire, and your response was ready to retaliate like a cannonball. In this age of technology, there are countless opportunities for mixed messages and misinterpreted text. The heart behind the message often gets lost because the words are confined to text, missing the sweet melody of the spoken word. When we're in a hurry, our best intentions can be marred by haste, leading to misunderstood phrases and quick reactions.

As we go about our days, let us strive to increase our ability to listen with grace and compassion, while decreasing the speed with which we take offense or respond hastily in anger. We must remember that our profession requires compassion, humility, and grace. While we are encouraged to show grace to others, often the person most in need of grace is ourselves. Let us take a moment to offer grace to ourselves for our perceived imperfections and failures, just as we work to encourage others when they miss the mark or offended by words or actions. James reminds us to be quick to listen, slow to speak, and slow to become angry. This posture allows God's mercy and grace to be reflected in our lives, as we grow in self-control and discipline.

Prayer:

Heavenly Father,
I know how easy it is to be offended and quickly prepare a response that sets the record straight with a sharp tongue or condescending remark. Yet, You have commanded us to be still. Lord, I ask for Your forgiveness for the times I've responded quickly in anger. Grant me Your peace to remain still in situations where I feel offended, and bring James 1:19 to my mind as a reminder to be quick to listen, slow to speak, and slow to become angry. I know that through Your strength, I can make subtle changes that will make me more like You. Thank You for the gift of grace that I can receive and give to others. Guard my words and actions today as I desire to live according to the directions in Your Holy Word. I receive a renewed mind and spirit.

In Jesus' name. Amen!

James 1:19 (NIV)

My dear brothers and sisters, take note of this: Everyone should be quick to listen, slow to speak, and slow to become angry.

Reflection and Prayer

Week of _____

Sunday:

_____

_____

Monday:

_____

_____

Tuesday:

_____

_____

Wednesday:

_____

_____

Thursday:

_____

_____

Friday:

_____

_____

Saturday:

_____

_____

	Sunday	Monday	Tuesday
3:00 - 4:00			
4:00 - 5:00			
5:00 - 6:00			
6:00 - 7:00			
7:00 - 8:00			
8:00 - 9:00			
9:00 - 10:00			
10:00 - 11:00			
11:00 - 12:00			
12:00 - 1:00			
1:00 - 2:00			
2:00 - 3:00			
3:00 - 4:00			
4:00 - 5:00			
5:00 - 6:00			
6:00 - 7:00			
7:00 - 8:00			

Wednesday	Thursday	Friday	Saturday

Week 3
Chosen

What does it mean to be chosen? How does it feel to be chosen? Think back to childhood during gym class, or in the neighborhood, waiting to be picked for a kickball, football, basketball, or baseball team. Or, more recently, think about a situation where you were selected to represent an organization, participate in a special project, or lead a team. What feelings accompanied that selection? Was it pride, joy, a sense of belonging, acceptance, or recognition? The list of emotions could go on.

That same longing to be chosen finds its fulfillment in Christ. Our Almighty and sovereign God has chosen us to be His hands, feet, and heart on this earth. Despite what happens in our homes, classrooms, cafeterias, gymnasiums, or offices, we should walk with purpose, knowing that we are God's chosen people. We are loved by God, and in turn, we are called to treat others with the same love, compassion, kindness, gentleness, humility, and patience that God so freely gives us. In difficult, tense, or less-than-perfect situations, let us be reminded that we are clothed with holiness, love, and kindness, living as representatives of the love of Jesus here on earth.

Prayer:

Dear God,
I am less than perfect, yet You chose me to demonstrate a life of holiness, compassion, kindness, humility, gentleness, and patience. You knew I couldn't do it on my own, so You gave Your Son as a sacrifice, to cover my sins. As I live to honor You, strengthen me when I am weak and direct me when I am misguided or off track. Today is a new day, and I choose to live in a manner that reflects the attributes You placed within me when You chose me. I am grateful for Your love, guidance, and faith in me to accomplish the tasks You've assigned to me. Help me to see beyond the clouds on dark days, knowing You provided Your "Sonlight" to guide me. Bless me, Lord, as I seek to be a blessing to others.

In Jesus' name, Amen!

Colossians 3:12 (NIV)
Therefore, as God's chosen people, holy and dearly loved, clothe yourselves with compassion, kindness, humility, gentleness, and patience.

Reflection and Prayer

Week of _____

Sunday:

_____

_____

Monday:

_____

_____

Tuesday:

_____

_____

Wednesday:

_____

_____

Thursday:

_____

_____

Friday:

_____

_____

Saturday:

_____

_____

	Sunday	Monday	Tuesday
3:00 - 4:00			
4:00 - 5:00			
5:00 - 6:00			
6:00 - 7:00			
7:00 - 8:00			
8:00 - 9:00			
9:00 - 10:00			
10:00 - 11:00			
11:00 - 12:00			
12:00 - 1:00			
1:00 - 2:00			
2:00 - 3:00			
3:00 - 4:00			
4:00 - 5:00			
5:00 - 6:00			
6:00 - 7:00			
7:00 - 8:00			

Wednesday	Thursday	Friday	Saturday

Week 4
Priorities

One more lesson plan. One more assignment. One more test. One more field trip. One more professional development session. One more course. One more meeting. One more conference. One more performance. One more assembly. One more science project. One more athletic game. One more review. One more observation. With the endless list of "one mores", where do we make room for one more—time with God? Time to worship. Time to praise. Time to read. Time to pray.

With so many items on our to-do lists, we are commanded to seek God's kingdom first and His righteousness, and everything else will be added. When we feel there isn't enough time in the day to worship, read, or pray, we must remember that as we prioritize our relationship and time with God, He, in His infinite ability, will create the time we need to handle everything else. When we make time for God, His Kingdom, and His righteousness, He will add "all these things". Whatever it is, give it to God. As we prioritize time on our agenda and day with God, He will keep His promise to supply what we need. Committing Matthew 6:33 to memory helps in those moments when we struggle to find quiet time with God.

Prayer:

Dear God,
First, I ask for forgiveness for those times when the busyness of my day distracted me from spending time with You. As I learn to seek Your kingdom first, I pray that You continue to bless me with Your Spirit, to guide my thoughts, actions, words, and day. I have faith and believe in Your promises. Help me, Lord, to tithe not only my finances, but also my time to worship and serve You. Show me how I can begin or increase serving in Your kingdom. Also, show me how to prioritize and plan accordingly to increase both the quality and quantity of time I spend with You each day. Please continue to bless the work of my hands and heart as I enhance my personal relationship with You. I believe my prayers are already answered.

In Jesus' name, Amen!

Matthew 6:33 (NIV)
But seek first His kingdom and His righteousness, and all these things will be given to you as well.

Reflection and Prayer

Week of _____

Sunday:

_____

_____

Monday:

_____

_____

Tuesday:

_____

_____

Wednesday:

_____

_____

Thursday:

_____

_____

Friday:

_____

_____

Saturday:

_____

_____

	Sunday	Monday	Tuesday
3:00 - 4:00			
4:00 - 5:00			
5:00 - 6:00			
6:00 - 7:00			
7:00 - 8:00			
8:00 - 9:00			
9:00 - 10:00			
10:00 - 11:00			
11:00 - 12:00			
12:00 - 1:00			
1:00 - 2:00			
2:00 - 3:00			
3:00 - 4:00			
4:00 - 5:00			
5:00 - 6:00			
6:00 - 7:00			
7:00 - 8:00			

Wednesday	Thursday	Friday	Saturday

Month of_____

SUNDAY	MONDAY	TUESDAY	WEDNESDAY

THURSDAY	FRIDAY	SATURDAY	NOTES

Week 5

Kingdom Kids

In certain households, the innocence of childhood is preserved, and children enjoy carefree days filled with love, joy, peace, and laughter. These children expect toys for their birthdays, dinner on the table, an allowance for ice cream, a coat when it's cold, and a trip to a beautiful location when it's warm. For others, this lifestyle seems unimaginable. Instead, they share a bed or couch with a sibling or family member, experience cold nights with inadequate warmth, and rely on an older sibling or friend for care, while the sole provider works long hours to put food on the table and keep the electricity on for another week.

In Matthew 18:1, a disciple asked Jesus, "Who, then, is the greatest in the kingdom of heaven?" Jesus replied that whoever takes the lowly position of a child and welcomes a child in His name is the greatest in the kingdom. I pray that as we encounter individuals who appear to have less earthly wealth, we regard them as the greatest in the kingdom of Heaven. Let us use Matthew 18:5 as a reminder that when we welcome and love children, we are also welcoming Jesus.

Prayer:

Dear Lord,
How sweet it is to have what we need and extra. Please help me remember that not everyone has the basic necessities or luxuries, such as their own bed or a hot meal every night. As I go about my day, convict me when I am impatient with someone or cast judgment for their inability to complete a task or assignment. Remind me that when I provide love, care, and support to a child, I am offering that as a direct reflection of what I am offering to You, Jesus. Keep my heart pure and remove any judgmental thoughts or actions. I am grateful for all that I am blessed with, and I ask for Your blessing on someone I am thinking of right now who needs me to show more love, kindness, and support. Guard my heart and renew a right spirit within me. Help me to genuinely love and welcome all children in the same manner I seek to love and welcome You. I praise and bless Your name, Jesus. Amen!

Matthew 18:4-5

Therefore, whoever takes the lowly position of this child is the greatest in the kingdom of Heaven. And whoever welcomes one such child in my name welcomes me.

Reflection and Prayer

Week of _____

Sunday:
_____
_____

Monday:
_____
_____

Tuesday:
_____
_____

Wednesday:
_____
_____

Thursday:
_____
_____

Friday:
_____
_____

Saturday:
_____
_____

	Sunday	Monday	Tuesday
3:00 - 4:00			
4:00 - 5:00			
5:00 - 6:00			
6:00 - 7:00			
7:00 - 8:00			
8:00 - 9:00			
9:00 - 10:00			
10:00 - 11:00			
11:00 - 12:00			
12:00 - 1:00			
1:00 - 2:00			
2:00 - 3:00			
3:00 - 4:00			
4:00 - 5:00			
5:00 - 6:00			
6:00 - 7:00			
7:00 - 8:00			

Wednesday	Thursday	Friday	Saturday

Week 6

Overcomer

What a blessed day this is! This is the day the Lord has made, and I will rejoice and be glad in it. Why should I rejoice?

Because I am powerful.
I am confident.
I am committed.
I am a believer.
I am a conqueror.
I am a child of God.
I can do all things through Christ who strengthens me.

Today is the day I will slow down, appreciate my blessings, and assess my goals. What has God spoken to me? Am I working toward it? Have I achieved it? Am I moving the needle to the next marker? Life is about intentionality taking deliberate steps toward purposeful goals. One step at a time. One day at a time. Today, I affirm that I can and will do ALL things through Christ who strengthens me.

Prayer:

Dear God,

I thank You for the blessing of another day. Please guide my thoughts and actions as I move closer to attaining ALL the promises You have spoken over my life. I reject any thoughts, feelings, or actions that are not of You, and I turn away from anything that distracts me from fulfilling my purpose. I am Your child, and Your strength allows me to walk boldly into the purpose You have for me. I renew my commitment to You today, and I will take measurable steps toward reaching my next marker.

I thank You for Your Word, which reminds me that I can do all things through Your Son, Jesus Christ. I receive and walk in Your promise, knowing that Your power gives me the strength to overcome any challenge.

In Jesus' name, Amen!

Philippians 4:13 (KJV)
I can do all things through Christ who strengthens me

Reflection and Prayer

Week of _____

Sunday:

_____

_____

Monday:

_____

_____

Tuesday:

_____

_____

Wednesday:

_____

_____

Thursday:

_____

_____

Friday:

_____

_____

Saturday:

_____

_____

	Sunday	Monday	Tuesday
3:00 - 4:00			
4:00 - 5:00			
5:00 - 6:00			
6:00 - 7:00			
7:00 - 8:00			
8:00 - 9:00			
9:00 - 10:00			
10:00 - 11:00			
11:00 - 12:00			
12:00 - 1:00			
1:00 - 2:00			
2:00 - 3:00			
3:00 - 4:00			
4:00 - 5:00			
5:00 - 6:00			
6:00 - 7:00			
7:00 - 8:00			

Wednesday	Thursday	Friday	Saturday

Week 7
Release and Lean

As we go through life, we encounter situations that seem to get the best of us—a family member is ill, a misunderstanding with a dear friend, we aren't offered a new position, and another meeting is scheduled. As these events swirl in our minds, it's easy to get lost in the unfortunate realities they bring. However, God reminds us to cast all our cares on Him because He cares about you (1 Peter 5:7). We must do our best to let go of anything that keeps us trapped in a cycle of despair or negativity. Learning to release our burdens and lean into God can loosen the grip of thoughts that ensnare us, like a web, keeping us from moving forward. Releasing and leaning in allows us to transfer the weight to the One who is able to bear it, as we persevere and run the race He has already set before us.

Prayer:

Dear God,

We are created in Your image. Deliver me from anything that hinders me from hearing Your voice. Remove the gray areas in my life that sometimes allow me to slip into darkness. Keep me on the straight and narrow path that leads me to You, with my actions, words, and thoughts aligned to Your will. Grant me the strength and endurance to run the race You've laid out for me. Provide me with living water when I grow thirsty along this journey, so that I can keep my eyes on You and the ultimate prize of eternal life.

Lord, You are my strength and guide. Allow me to rest in Your arms when I grow tired. Protect me from the schemes of the enemy and keep my armor intact as I serve You. Thank You that the victory has already been won, because You are always there to fight my battles. Restore my faith when it is weak, and surround me with individuals who will encourage me to choose the right path over the easy one.

In Jesus's name, Amen.

Hebrews 12:1 (NIV)
Therefore, since we are surrounded by such a great cloud of witnesses, let us throw off everything that hinders and the sin that so easily entangles. And let us run with perseverance the race marked out for us.

Reflection and Prayer

Week of _____

Sunday:

_____

_____

Monday:

_____

_____

Tuesday:

_____

_____

Wednesday:

_____

_____

Thursday:

_____

_____

Friday:

_____

_____

Saturday:

_____

_____

	Sunday	Monday	Tuesday
3:00 - 4:00			
4:00 - 5:00			
5:00 - 6:00			
6:00 - 7:00			
7:00 - 8:00			
8:00 - 9:00			
9:00 - 10:00			
10:00 - 11:00			
11:00 - 12:00			
12:00 - 1:00			
1:00 - 2:00			
2:00 - 3:00			
3:00 - 4:00			
4:00 - 5:00			
5:00 - 6:00			
6:00 - 7:00			
7:00 - 8:00			

Wednesday	Thursday	Friday	Saturday

Week 8
Rest in the Shadows

There are times, we work ourselves into exhaustion. We start before the sun rises, working tirelessly without a break throughout the day, then taking a few moments to rest before starting all over again. Our bodies were not designed to push through life without resting. Sometimes, God takes a moment to remind us that He is leading us on our journey. While society creates the need for more, due to earthly comparisons, we should strive for more, with the goal of being completely poured out when pursuing God's promises given to us in His word. God reminds us of the talents we have been given and He expects a return on His investment, but He also provides a place of shelter where we can rest comfortably, knowing that He will provide all of our needs. As we begin this day, let's be intentional about finding balance. Balance can be attained by being a good steward of the talents God expects us to use and multiply, but also by stopping and resting as a sign of surrender in believing God is able to rejuvenate and restore us just as He rested on the seventh day.

Prayer:

Dear God,

I come to You right now asking for forgiveness. Lord, I recognize how the pace of this world pushes me to constantly want more. Please guide me and bless me with the discernment to stop and rest in Your shadow, where I am safe and can be refreshed. Teach me to pause long enough to hear from You, free from distractions. I want to be still, to hear Your voice and Your directions. I ask that You bless my day and order my steps so that I am obedient to Your will. Thank You for providing a place of refuge where I can shelter from life's storms and rest.

In Jesus's name, Amen.

Psalm 91:1 (NIV)
Whoever dwells in the shelter of the Most High will rest in the shadow of the Almighty.

Reflection and Prayer

Week of _____

Sunday:

_____

_____

Monday:

_____

_____

Tuesday:

_____

_____

Wednesday:

_____

_____

Thursday:

_____

_____

Friday:

_____

_____

Saturday:

_____

_____

	Sunday	Monday	Tuesday
3:00 - 4:00			
4:00 - 5:00			
5:00 - 6:00			
6:00 - 7:00			
7:00 - 8:00			
8:00 - 9:00			
9:00 - 10:00			
10:00 - 11:00			
11:00 - 12:00			
12:00 - 1:00			
1:00 - 2:00			
2:00 - 3:00			
3:00 - 4:00			
4:00 - 5:00			
5:00 - 6:00			
6:00 - 7:00			
7:00 - 8:00			

Wednesday	Thursday	Friday	Saturday

Month of_____

SUNDAY	MONDAY	TUESDAY	WEDNESDAY

THURSDAY	FRIDAY	SATURDAY	NOTES

Week 9

Woe to Worship

How we handle challenges varies from person to person. One person might draw closer to God during a challenging life experience while another may drift away while questioning the "why" and "who" of the experience. As we encounter life's trials, we must always remember that the Lord our God is with us. Not only is He with us, but the same spirit that raised Jesus from the dead (Romans 6:10) lives in us as well. We have the power to overcome life's challenges. We must be intentional about calling on the name of the Lord in times of trouble. Actively praising Him and giving thanks for all the great things He has done in our lives shifts the focus from woe to worship. The Lord delights in us and rejoices with us as we overcome challenges. Let us shift from silent to vocal praise and lift our voices out loud to praise, worship and glorify the mighty name of Jesus.

Please pray out loud.

Dear God,
I come to You with my arms wide open. I lift my hands to worship. I lift my voice to praise and glorify Your name. As I begin this day, I choose to intentionally shift my words from woe to worship. I speak life in the name of Jesus. I know You are with me, Lord, and You have saved me from a life of worry, lack, and complaining. Right now, I thank You for Your love and for blessing me with another day to praise Your name. I give You my worries, concerns, and fears, and I receive Your peace, joy, and love. Bless me throughout this day, and may Your presence lead me in all I do.

In Jesus's name, Amen.

Zephaniah 3:17 (NIV)

The Lord your God is with you, the Mighty Warrior who saves. He will take great delight in you; in His love, He will no longer rebuke you but will rejoice over you with singing.

.

Reflection and Prayer

Week of _____

Sunday:

_____

_____

Monday:

_____

_____

Tuesday:

_____

_____

Wednesday:

_____

_____

Thursday:

_____

_____

Friday:

_____

_____

Saturday:

_____

_____

	Sunday	Monday	Tuesday
3:00 - 4:00			
4:00 - 5:00			
5:00 - 6:00			
6:00 - 7:00			
7:00 - 8:00			
8:00 - 9:00			
9:00 - 10:00			
10:00 - 11:00			
11:00 - 12:00			
12:00 - 1:00			
1:00 - 2:00			
2:00 - 3:00			
3:00 - 4:00			
4:00 - 5:00			
5:00 - 6:00			
6:00 - 7:00			
7:00 - 8:00			

Wednesday	Thursday	Friday	Saturday

Week 10
I am CHOSEN

During Bible study, the group leader asked, "When did you choose God?" I responded, "I didn't choose God; God chose me." Little did I know, one of the verses prepared for the study was John 15:16. In that moment, God confirmed in my spirit that I was chosen. As educators, we know we are chosen for this profession. It's not the pay or the "summers off" as many believe. It is the heart for our students and community that drives us, even when we feel we have nothing left to give. As we begin this day, let's walk with confidence, knowing we are chosen and equipped for the assignment God has given us.

Prayer:

Dear Lord,
I am asking for Your guidance and strength today. Thank You for choosing me to lead and love the students and community You have placed me in. I walk in Your strength as I begin this day. Because I am chosen, I trust that whatever challenges I face today, You have already gone before me. I place any fears, worries, or anxiety at Your feet and walk away with the strength to overcome whatever arises. Thank You for choosing me. It is my heart's desire to do my best and to please You in all that I do. Grant me the discernment to make the right decisions and the confidence to stand firm in Your truth.

In Jesus' name, Amen.

John 15:16 (KJV)
You did not choose me, but I chose you and appointed you so that you might go and bear fruit—fruit that will last—and so that whatever you ask in my name the Father will give you.

Reflection and Prayer

Week of _____

Sunday:

_____

_____

Monday:

_____

_____

Tuesday:

_____

_____

Wednesday:

_____

_____

Thursday:

_____

_____

Friday:

_____

_____

Saturday:

_____

_____

	Sunday	Monday	Tuesday
3:00 - 4:00			
4:00 - 5:00			
5:00 - 6:00			
6:00 - 7:00			
7:00 - 8:00			
8:00 - 9:00			
9:00 - 10:00			
10:00 - 11:00			
11:00 - 12:00			
12:00 - 1:00			
1:00 - 2:00			
2:00 - 3:00			
3:00 - 4:00			
4:00 - 5:00			
5:00 - 6:00			
6:00 - 7:00			
7:00 - 8:00			

Wednesday	Thursday	Friday	Saturday

Week 11
God is Faithful

How do we handle delayed responses to prayers? As we go through this day, let us hold on to the hope that God hears our prayers and answers in His time, because He knows best—whether the answer is yes, no, or not yet. Since He knows what's best for us, our own experiences or expectations might lead us down the wrong path. His Word tells us He will grant us the desires of our hearts, but we cannot be disappointed when He places His desires in our hearts, shifting our plans. Let us ask God to reveal the desires He intends for us as we begin this day, striving to fulfill His purpose in our lives. We must not stop hoping, because He is faithful.

Prayer:

Dear God,
I thank You for being true to Your word and for fulfilling Your promises. Your word says that God is not a man that He should lie (Numbers 23:19), therefore, we must stand firmly on Your promises, not swerving or doubting while we wait. Help us to hold tightly to Your mighty right hand as You lead us through life. We thank You, Lord, for Your unwavering faithfulness. Strengthen, guide, and comfort us as we wait on You.

In Jesus' name we pray, Amen.

Hebrews 10:23 (NIV)
Let us hold unswervingly to the hope we profess, for He who promised is faithful.

Reflection and Prayer

Week of _____

Sunday:

_____

_____

Monday:

_____

_____

Tuesday:

_____

_____

Wednesday:

_____

_____

Thursday:

_____

_____

Friday:

_____

_____

Saturday:

_____

_____

	Sunday	Monday	Tuesday
3:00 - 4:00			
4:00 - 5:00			
5:00 - 6:00			
6:00 - 7:00			
7:00 - 8:00			
8:00 - 9:00			
9:00 - 10:00			
10:00 - 11:00			
11:00 - 12:00			
12:00 - 1:00			
1:00 - 2:00			
2:00 - 3:00			
3:00 - 4:00			
4:00 - 5:00			
5:00 - 6:00			
6:00 - 7:00			
7:00 - 8:00			

Wednesday	Thursday	Friday	Saturday

Week 12
A Heart to Serve

As educators, we begin and end our days knowing that we are in an environment of service and protection. As our students fill our halls and classrooms, we are prepared to offer more than just academic lessons. We provide relational, familial, social, physiological, and mental support. When we first entered the field of education, we didn't fully understand the depth of the strength required to walk daily into a familiar environment, only to face unknown scenarios every day. As we start this day, let us give God praise in advance for the strength and wisdom He provides as we navigate whatever challenges or situations we encounter throughout the day.

Prayer:

Dear God,

Thank You for providing the strength we need daily to fulfill Your purpose in our lives through the students, parents, community, faculty, and staff we serve. Grant us the strength of David, to overcome the giants that seek to slow us down or hinder us from being victorious in our challenges. Thank You for securing our paths and empowering us with Your strength. We will sing Your praises like David.

In Jesus' name. Amen.

2 Samuel 22:33 (NIV)

"It is God who arms me with strength and keeps my way secure."

Reflection and Prayer

Week of _____

Sunday:

_____

_____

Monday:

_____

_____

Tuesday:

_____

_____

Wednesday:

_____

_____

Thursday:

_____

_____

Friday:

_____

_____

Saturday:

_____

_____

	Sunday	Monday	Tuesday
3:00 - 4:00			
4:00 - 5:00			
5:00 - 6:00			
6:00 - 7:00			
7:00 - 8:00			
8:00 - 9:00			
9:00 - 10:00			
10:00 - 11:00			
11:00 - 12:00			
12:00 - 1:00			
1:00 - 2:00			
2:00 - 3:00			
3:00 - 4:00			
4:00 - 5:00			
5:00 - 6:00			
6:00 - 7:00			
7:00 - 8:00			

Wednesday	Thursday	Friday	Saturday

Month of_____

SUNDAY	MONDAY	TUESDAY	WEDNESDAY

THURSDAY	FRIDAY	SATURDAY	NOTES

Week 13
God's Masterpiece

Although our profession requires us to lead, uplift, and inspire others, there are times when we are the ones in need of guidance and inspiration. When deadlines loom, parents have demands, students have questions, and the pressure feels overwhelming, it's in these moments that we need a gentle reminder: we were created for this specific time to plant, nourish, and water the seeds placed in our garden. That garden may be a classroom, cafeteria, art or music room, gymnasium, or STEM lab. The location doesn't matter—what matters is how we nurture the seeds entrusted to us, making the garden unique and special. As we tend to our "gardens", let us do our best to remove the weeds of negativity and doubt that try to overpower the beautiful flowers that are waiting to bloom. Despite challenges and differences, we must declare, "I am fearfully and wonderfully made; Your works are wonderful, I know that full well."

Prayer:

Dear God,
Thank You for this moment in time. Right now, You are reminding me that You created a masterpiece when You knitted me together in my mother's womb. Even when I feel inadequate or unprepared in the face of life's challenges, I thank You for Your renewed reminder that I am created in Your perfect image; therefore, I am a unique and priceless work of art. Renew my mind, strengthen my spirit, and restore the confidence, peace, love, and joy that You sealed within me. Lord, I am so grateful for this reminder today. I will walk boldly in the authority You placed within me. Strengthen me when I am weak. Comfort me when I feel alone. Guide me when I feel lost. Inspire me when I feel hopeless. I speak renewed life, passion, and purpose into this day. I believe it is done.

In Jesus' mighty name. Amen!

Psalm 139:13-14 (NIV)

For you created my inmost being; you knit me together in my mother's womb. I praise you because I am fearfully and wonderfully made; your works are wonderful, I know that full well.

Reflection and Prayer

Week of _____

Sunday:

_____

_____

Monday:

_____

_____

Tuesday:

_____

_____

Wednesday:

_____

_____

Thursday:

_____

_____

Friday:

_____

_____

Saturday:

_____

_____

	Sunday	Monday	Tuesday
3:00 - 4:00			
4:00 - 5:00			
5:00 - 6:00			
6:00 - 7:00			
7:00 - 8:00			
8:00 - 9:00			
9:00 - 10:00			
10:00 - 11:00			
11:00 - 12:00			
12:00 - 1:00			
1:00 - 2:00			
2:00 - 3:00			
3:00 - 4:00			
4:00 - 5:00			
5:00 - 6:00			
6:00 - 7:00			
7:00 - 8:00			

Wednesday	Thursday	Friday	Saturday

Week 14
Transform and Renew

What a significant day it has been! I woke up early, listened to C.S. Lewis, and was led to a passage of scripture by God that echoed the same theme of being chosen as a "watchman". Wow, how am I supposed to process this assignment? In this same way, our students are tasked with digesting new or unfamiliar information, with the ultimate goal of increasing their understanding so it can be effectively applied. As believers, God calls us to lean in and listen for His voice. Just as we sometimes need the individuals we instruct, or lead, to be quiet, God also has those moments with us, where He is calling us to silence, so we can hear from Him. What are His directions? What steps should we take? How do we know if we're on the right path? Should we expect a nod or confirmation to assure us that we've heard the right answer?

As we pray, part of our posture should include moments of silence to listen for God's guidance or Holy Spirit's presence, followed by time to meditate and process what we've heard, before stepping out to put it into action. Today, let us ask God to transform and renew our hearts and minds as we seek to serve Him and allow His light to shine, so others may be encouraged to trust in Him as their Lord and Savior.

Prayer:

El Shaddai, Lord Almighty,
I come to You with a humble heart, asking for Your guidance. Grant me the strength to accept the truth that I am Holy (set apart). Transform and renew my mind, aligning my thoughts with Your thoughts and my ways with Your ways. Bless me with Your spirit as I go through this day. Remind me, when things don't go as planned, that You are in control and my steps are ordered by You. Thank You in advance for giving me victory in every area of my day. Bless my students, friends, family, coworkers, administrators, and leaders. Grant me Your wisdom and understanding. Allow me to be effective in everything I do today.

I receive it in Jesus' mighty name. Amen!

Romans 12:2 (NIV)

Do not conform to the pattern of this world, but be transformed by the renewing of your mind. Then you will be able to test and approve what God's will is—his good, pleasing and perfect will.

Reflection and Prayer

Week of _____

Sunday:

_____
_____

Monday:

_____
_____

Tuesday:

_____
_____

Wednesday:

_____
_____

Thursday:

_____
_____

Friday:

_____
_____

Saturday:

_____
_____

	Sunday	Monday	Tuesday
3:00 - 4:00			
4:00 - 5:00			
5:00 - 6:00			
6:00 - 7:00			
7:00 - 8:00			
8:00 - 9:00			
9:00 - 10:00			
10:00 - 11:00			
11:00 - 12:00			
12:00 - 1:00			
1:00 - 2:00			
2:00 - 3:00			
3:00 - 4:00			
4:00 - 5:00			
5:00 - 6:00			
6:00 - 7:00			
7:00 - 8:00			

Wednesday	Thursday	Friday	Saturday

Week 15
Surrender

When we consider the role of an educator in any capacity, we must marvel at the skills required to enter, sustain, and thrive in this profession—or as many call it, "our calling". God has blessed us with indescribable gifts. The ability to nurture, instruct, love, discipline, redirect, and lead are just a few of these gifts. The ability to support a class of any size requires a level of organization, patience, and talent that is often hard to explain to those beyond the walls of education. In education, we are asked to lead a group of diverse personalities, abilities, and cultures, guiding them down a differentiated but similar path. Our global systems depend on educators. Whether it's in a daycare center, elementary, middle, high school, college, or professional level, educators are essential in pushing individuals beyond their perceived abilities and propelling them to the next level.

Just as Daniel thanked God for wisdom, as educators, we must also give thanks for the wisdom and power God has bestowed on us. We are not successful by our strength; it is God gracefully answering our prayers when He makes known to us what we ask of Him. He shows us that with Him, all things are possible. This is the daily reminder we need as we boldly enter our arena, seeking God to grant us wisdom and make His ways known to us. We ask that He guides our words, softens our hearts, builds our confidence, protects our spaces, and helps us deliver life-changing lessons that will introduce our students to a new world, guiding them from success to success. As we go about today, let us be reminded that God grants us the wisdom and power not just to survive, but to thrive.

Prayer:

Dear God,
I come to You, first to say, "Thank You." Thank You for speaking to me directly and guiding me with Your mighty right hand. Thank You for giving me the wisdom to lead and the power to be courageous in the face of fear, anxiety, and uncertainty. Right now, in the name of Jesus, I release anything that holds me back from living my best life in You, and I accept all that You have assigned to me to complete today. Lord, please forgive me for doubting myself, but more so for doubting You. I know You hear me, and You are waiting for my "Yes" and "Surrender." Right now, I give everything to You. I will walk upright in Your promises over my life, letting the past fall behind me. I release any thoughts of failure, past mistakes, or personal judgment, and I am picking up the beautiful pieces of my life to create Your masterpiece. I speak life, victory, healing, abundance, salvation, and freedom right now.

In Jesus' mighty name. Amen!

Daniel 2:23 (NIV)

"I thank and praise you, God of my ancestors: You have given me wisdom and power, you have made known to me what we asked of you, you have made known to us the dream of the king."

Reflection and Prayer

Week of _____

Sunday:
_____
_____

Monday:
_____
_____

Tuesday:
_____
_____

Wednesday:
_____
_____

Thursday:
_____
_____

Friday:
_____
_____

Saturday:
_____
_____

	Sunday	Monday	Tuesday
3:00 - 4:00			
4:00 - 5:00			
5:00 - 6:00			
6:00 - 7:00			
7:00 - 8:00			
8:00 - 9:00			
9:00 - 10:00			
10:00 - 11:00			
11:00 - 12:00			
12:00 - 1:00			
1:00 - 2:00			
2:00 - 3:00			
3:00 - 4:00			
4:00 - 5:00			
5:00 - 6:00			
6:00 - 7:00			
7:00 - 8:00			

Wednesday	Thursday	Friday	Saturday

Week 16
A Fixed Gaze

As we begin our day, it's easy to become distracted when the unexpected arises. We may encounter a hurting child, a disgruntled parent, a less-than-favorable review, or a new program. If we are not grounded, it's all too easy to lose sight of our objective, the goals for the day, or the great things God has already done. We must remember to keep our eyes on the Lord. He orders our steps, protects our paths, graces us with wisdom, and showers us with love. No matter what arises, we must not be shaken, for the Lord is taking us by the hand and walking with us every step of the way.

Prayer:

Dear Lord,
Every day brings scenarios I've encountered before, or something completely new. As I embrace the beauty of this new day, please continue to grip my hand tightly. When I feel overwhelmed or the weight becomes too heavy, steady my stance and lead me to solid ground where I cannot be shaken. No matter what swirls around me, I will keep my eyes on You and regain my footing. Just as Peter walked on water as long as he kept his eyes on You, I, too, will fix my gaze only on You, so that I can walk on water and make it to the other side.

Psalm 16:8 (NIV)

I keep my eyes always on the Lord, with him at my right hand, I will not be shaken.

Reflection and Prayer

Week of _____

Sunday:

_____

_____

Monday:

_____

_____

Tuesday:

_____

_____

Wednesday:

_____

_____

Thursday:

_____

_____

Friday:

_____

_____

Saturday:

_____

_____

	Sunday	Monday	Tuesday
3:00 - 4:00			
4:00 - 5:00			
5:00 - 6:00			
6:00 - 7:00			
7:00 - 8:00			
8:00 - 9:00			
9:00 - 10:00			
10:00 - 11:00			
11:00 - 12:00			
12:00 - 1:00			
1:00 - 2:00			
2:00 - 3:00			
3:00 - 4:00			
4:00 - 5:00			
5:00 - 6:00			
6:00 - 7:00			
7:00 - 8:00			

Wednesday	Thursday	Friday	Saturday

Month of_____

SUNDAY	MONDAY	TUESDAY	WEDNESDAY

THURSDAY	FRIDAY	SATURDAY	NOTES

Week 17
Committed to My Assignment

We all know that feeling. An event occurs, and suddenly, a student is upset, a parent is frustrated, a peer is conflicted, and a supervisor must step in to resolve the situation—only for the resolution to not align with your perspective or response. We've all experienced moments where we felt unsupported, as though our feelings weren't considered, or our decisions weren't valued. Sometimes, frustration gets the best of us, and we lose sight of what's truly important. In these moments, we must remember that how communication and problems are handled can serve as a real-life example for those around us.

This is God's reminder to you today: No matter what today looks like, and no matter how dim your light feels right now, don't let someone else's actions pull you away from the assignment God gave you. Your students, friends, family, and peers need the guidance, love, instruction, and motivation that only you can provide. There will always be obstacles in our paths and mountains to climb, but God reminds us that He will never leave us or forsake us (Hebrews 13:5). God orders our steps, and expects us to remain still until He directs us to our next assignment. Just as He asked the disciples in Matthew 26:40 to stay awake and pray, He is asking us to stay committed, despite the trials. God says in Jeremiah 29:11, "I know the plans I have for you, plans to prosper you and not to harm you, plans to give you a hope and a future."

Prayer:

Dear God,
I come to You, asking for forgiveness for the thoughts I've allowed to creep into my mind. I'm sorry for allowing someone else's directions to remove or dampen the joy and peace You've placed within me. Lord, give me the strength to joyfully serve in Your kingdom, despite the difficulties I encounter. Holy Spirit, when I am tempted to give up, please remind me that this is a temporary moment, and I can do all things through Christ who strengthens me (Philippians 4:13). Thank You for speaking to me today. I receive Your strength to keep going.

In Jesus' name, Amen.

Ecclesiastes 10:4 (NIV)

If a ruler's anger rises against you, do not leave your post; calmness can lay great offenses to rest.

Reflection and Prayer

Week of _____

Sunday:

_____

_____

Monday:

_____

_____

Tuesday:

_____

_____

Wednesday:

_____

_____

Thursday:

_____

_____

Friday:

_____

_____

Saturday:

_____

_____

	Sunday	Monday	Tuesday
3:00 - 4:00			
4:00 - 5:00			
5:00 - 6:00			
6:00 - 7:00			
7:00 - 8:00			
8:00 - 9:00			
9:00 - 10:00			
10:00 - 11:00			
11:00 - 12:00			
12:00 - 1:00			
1:00 - 2:00			
2:00 - 3:00			
3:00 - 4:00			
4:00 - 5:00			
5:00 - 6:00			
6:00 - 7:00			
7:00 - 8:00			

Wednesday	Thursday	Friday	Saturday

Week 18
Everyone Stumbles

As educators, how often do we find ourselves reminding students that it's okay to make a mistake? Why is it so easy to extend grace to others but so hard to offer the same grace to ourselves? We work in a profession that's constantly measured by data, growth, and improvement. Formative, summative, and diagnostic assessments are always there, reminding us of how close or far we are from meeting or exceeding expectations. Yet, we should be grateful that our Heavenly Father is right there to hold us up with His mighty hand when we stumble or fall short. He doesn't pull up a graph, score sheet, or historical data to show how many times we've been less than perfect. Instead, He simply holds us by the hand, leading us to our next assignment or giving us another chance to improve on the current one.

As you go through this day, be reminded that we serve a God of second, third and more chances. He is not looking down to point out our flaws; rather, He is stretching out His hand to uplift us.

Prayer:

Dear Father,

Thank You for another day to get it right. Although there are moments when I feel like I've had more trials than victories, I am grateful for another day to walk hand in hand with You. Guide me when I'm wandering, and catch me when I feel like I'm falling. I walk securely, knowing that You are always with me. Even though I might stumble, I am thankful that You will not let me fall.

Psalms 37:23 (NIV)

The Lord makes firm the steps of the one who delights in Him; though he may stumble, he will not fall, for the Lord upholds him with His hand.

Reflection and Prayer

Week of _____

Sunday:

_____

_____

Monday:

_____

_____

Tuesday:

_____

_____

Wednesday:

_____

_____

Thursday:

_____

_____

Friday:

_____

_____

Saturday:

_____

_____

	Sunday	Monday	Tuesday
3:00 - 4:00			
4:00 - 5:00			
5:00 - 6:00			
6:00 - 7:00			
7:00 - 8:00			
8:00 - 9:00			
9:00 - 10:00			
10:00 - 11:00			
11:00 - 12:00			
12:00 - 1:00			
1:00 - 2:00			
2:00 - 3:00			
3:00 - 4:00			
4:00 - 5:00			
5:00 - 6:00			
6:00 - 7:00			
7:00 - 8:00			

Wednesday	Thursday	Friday	Saturday

Week 19
Choosing Humility

What does humility look like? There are times when we want our immediate needs met. We voice our concerns, but it feels like our words are falling on deaf ears. Our natural response might be to whine, complain, or share our frustrations with anyone who will listen. However, God gently reminds us to humble ourselves before Him, and He will lift us up. But what does that look like?

Sometimes, it means being quiet when we want to shout from the mountaintop. Sometimes, it means pausing to pray before we speak the words on our hearts. Other times, it might just take a soft hum of our favorite hymn or song that brings peace during a physical, mental, spiritual, or emotional storm. These actions require humility. They push us to rely on Jehovah Jireh for His provision in every area of our lives.

Let's work on intentionally choosing humility and peace as a body of believers, set apart in the way we handle disappointment, conflict, or confusion. God has given us an advocate and comforter who takes our petitions to the highest authority, always resolving our situations based on what's best for us. Let us rest, knowing that we serve a God who always supplies our needs.

Prayer:

Heavenly Father,
I come to You now, asking for forgiveness for the times I have chosen to take matters into my own hands. I ask for Your strength and guidance when I am weak and feel the urge to voice my opinions, seeking resolution. Help me, Lord, to choose humility as You've commanded. Remind me that I am humbling myself, not before earthly beings, but before my Heavenly Lord. Thank You for giving me another opportunity to choose peace, gentleness, compassion, and stillness in challenging situations. I stand on Your word and believe that You will honor my obedience and lift me up in every situation when I follow Your commands. Bless my heart, thoughts, words, and emotions right now. In Jesus' name, Amen!

James 4:10 (NIV)
Humble yourselves before the Lord, and He will lift you up.

Reflection and Prayer

Week of _____

Sunday:

_____

_____

Monday:

_____

_____

Tuesday:

_____

_____

Wednesday:

_____

_____

Thursday:

_____

_____

Friday:

_____

_____

Saturday:

_____

_____

	Sunday	Monday	Tuesday
3:00 - 4:00			
4:00 - 5:00			
5:00 - 6:00			
6:00 - 7:00			
7:00 - 8:00			
8:00 - 9:00			
9:00 - 10:00			
10:00 - 11:00			
11:00 - 12:00			
12:00 - 1:00			
1:00 - 2:00			
2:00 - 3:00			
3:00 - 4:00			
4:00 - 5:00			
5:00 - 6:00			
6:00 - 7:00			
7:00 - 8:00			

Wednesday	Thursday	Friday	Saturday

Week 20
The Ultimate Counselor

We are often presented with situations that require us to respond, lead, instruct, and interact with students, parents, administrators, or community members. As educators or supporters, we are frequently faced with decisions of varying levels of importance. In every situation, our goal is to make the right or best decision based on the available options. When determining the best response or course of action, we should always present our requests to the Lord for His divine guidance.

As we spend more private time with our Heavenly Father, we become familiar with the sound of His voice, the presence of the Holy Spirit, and the supernatural covering of the blood of Jesus. As we present our petitions and seek guidance, we must seek God's wisdom with the faith that He hears and responds according to His will, always providing what is best for us. Let us intentionally create a space that allows us to stop and seek the Lord's counsel before any decision is made.

Prayer:

Dear God,
Thank You for always being available to me. I stand in need of guidance, wisdom, and counsel today. I know You will always do what's best for me, even when I think I have the answer. Please remind me, through the help of the Holy Spirit, to stop and ask for Your guidance when making any decision, no matter how big or small. I fully surrender to Your way, Your guidance, and Your direction when I present my petitions to You. Thank You for being a merciful God, constantly extending Your hand and keeping Your ear available to listen whenever I call on You. Help me hear Your voice clearly and immediately act on the response You download into my spirit so I can follow the path You have cleared for me.

As I seek a closer relationship with You, please grant me the ability to hear Your voice clearly and discern Your will in every area of my life. I am grateful for the prayers You are answering at this very moment. I believe it and receive it to be done, in Jesus' mighty name, Amen!

I Kings 22:5 (KJV)
But Jehoshaphat also said to the king of Israel, "First, seek the counsel of the Lord."

Reflection and Prayer

Week of _____

Sunday:

_____

_____

Monday:

_____

_____

Tuesday:

_____

_____

Wednesday:

_____

_____

Thursday:

_____

_____

Friday:

_____

_____

Saturday:

_____

_____

	Sunday	Monday	Tuesday
3:00 - 4:00			
4:00 - 5:00			
5:00 - 6:00			
6:00 - 7:00			
7:00 - 8:00			
8:00 - 9:00			
9:00 - 10:00			
10:00 - 11:00			
11:00 - 12:00			
12:00 - 1:00			
1:00 - 2:00			
2:00 - 3:00			
3:00 - 4:00			
4:00 - 5:00			
5:00 - 6:00			
6:00 - 7:00			
7:00 - 8:00			

Wednesday	Thursday	Friday	Saturday

Month of_____

SUNDAY	MONDAY	TUESDAY	WEDNESDAY

THURSDAY	FRIDAY	SATURDAY	NOTES

Week 21
Guaranteed Promises

When trials arise, how do you respond? Do you immediately choose to dwell on the negative and what didn't work, or do you focus on the positive and recall the many times God showed up? Focusing on prior positive experiences when surrounded by challenging situations requires intentionality. When life throws a curveball, how we respond determines what happens next. We can choose to keep our eyes on the "prize" God promised us, knowing that despite life's challenges, we can remain hopeful, or we can blink shrink back, magnifying the current situation into a harsh reality.

Let's choose to keep our eyes open and focus on God's promises as we stand at the plate, eagerly anticipating the next home run. When we hope without swerving, God is able to deliver the home run with bases loaded, exceeding our expectations and fulfilling His promises. He offers us an abundant life, peace that surpasses understanding, and the assurance that we will never be left or forsaken. When we hold on to these promises, we can be confident that we serve a faithful God who will deliver on His word if we keep our eyes on Him and our hearts pure.

Prayer:

Dear God,
As Your child, I ask for forgiveness for the times I've taken my eyes off the ball and lost sight of what's ahead of me. Help me to stand firm when life throws an unexpected curveball. Bring back to my remembrance all the times You've provided for me, along with the reminder in Your word that You are faithful in keeping Your promises. Bless me today with the gift of perseverance, steadfastness, and the ability to keep my covenant with You. Help me to be bold in the midst of adversity, being a living example of what it means to fully trust that You will supply all my needs according to Your riches in glory (Philippians 4:19). You are a wonderful Father, and I thank You for my past, current, and future blessings that are still in store. I speak and receive it as done, in Jesus' mighty name. Amen.

Hebrews 10:23 (NIV)
Let us hold unswervingly to the hope we profess, for He who promised is faithful.

Reflection and Prayer

Week of _____

Sunday:

_____

_____

Monday:

_____

_____

Tuesday:

_____

_____

Wednesday:

_____

_____

Thursday:

_____

_____

Friday:

_____

_____

Saturday:

_____

_____

	Sunday	Monday	Tuesday
3:00 - 4:00			
4:00 - 5:00			
5:00 - 6:00			
6:00 - 7:00			
7:00 - 8:00			
8:00 - 9:00			
9:00 - 10:00			
10:00 - 11:00			
11:00 - 12:00			
12:00 - 1:00			
1:00 - 2:00			
2:00 - 3:00			
3:00 - 4:00			
4:00 - 5:00			
5:00 - 6:00			
6:00 - 7:00			
7:00 - 8:00			

Wednesday	Thursday	Friday	Saturday

Week 22
Early in the Morning

How many times do we wake up early in the morning, hoping, wishing, and praying to fall back asleep? We've probably experienced this more than we care to admit. But instead of trying our best to go back to sleep, what if we took that time to fellowship with God and ask our Advocate, Holy Spirit, to intercede on our behalf during these early mornings, to submit our requests and petitions to God.

In the Bible, we read about the times Jesus went away early in the morning to pray. Early morning isolation and prayer brings clarity that's usually more difficult to receive during the busyness of our days. Let's take a few moments to first thank God for seeing another day. Secondly, we can express our gratitude for all the blessings we have. We can then continue by praying for others, asking God to bless, cover, and protect our family, friends, coworkers, administrators, students, community, leaders, and our nation.

At this time of morning, we have a direct, quiet, and peaceful connection with God. We are able to sit silently and hear God's voice, allowing Him to download our assignments for the day with confidence. Let's practice being intentional about switching our early morning requests from continued sleep to moments of prayer, devotion, affirmations, and guidance for the day ahead.

Prayer:

Dear Lord,
How great Thou art! I thank You for another day. I am grateful for the times You've intentionally woken me up early to spend time with You before the distractions of the world. Lord, help me to go directly to You before checking my phone, emails, social media, or even the television. You are Jehovah Jireh, my Provider, and I thank You for Your provision.

As I begin another day, I don't know what lies ahead, but I ask for Your protection over our students, administrators, coworkers and community leaders. Lord, allow me to instruct, lead, and/or guide in a way that is pleasing to You. As prayed in 1 Kings 3:9, "Give Your servant a discerning heart to govern Your people and distinguish between right and wrong."

I thank You for hearing my voice and answering my prayers. Please continue to grant me Your grace, mercy, favor, wisdom, and understanding as I go through this day. I declare it, speak it, and believe it to be done.

In Jesus' name – Amen!

Psalm 5:3 (NIV)
In the morning, Lord, You hear my voice; in the morning, I lay my requests before You.

Reflection and Prayer

Week of _____

Sunday:

_____

_____

Monday:

_____

_____

Tuesday:

_____

_____

Wednesday:

_____

_____

Thursday:

_____

_____

Friday:

_____

_____

Saturday:

_____

_____

	Sunday	Monday	Tuesday
3:00 - 4:00			
4:00 - 5:00			
5:00 - 6:00			
6:00 - 7:00			
7:00 - 8:00			
8:00 - 9:00			
9:00 - 10:00			
10:00 - 11:00			
11:00 - 12:00			
12:00 - 1:00			
1:00 - 2:00			
2:00 - 3:00			
3:00 - 4:00			
4:00 - 5:00			
5:00 - 6:00			
6:00 - 7:00			
7:00 - 8:00			

Wednesday	Thursday	Friday	Saturday

Week 23
Fruit Bearers

I believe we all have some level of gardener within us. We may shy away from being called gardeners due to unsuccessful attempts at growing or keeping greenery alive. Yet, God reminds us that we are extensions of all that He is—grace, joy, love, peace, longsuffering, gentleness, patience, and self-control. We have all encountered difficult students, parents, administrators, coworkers, staff members, and even community members. When faced with challenging interactions, unflattering feedback, or unpleasant people, it's sometimes difficult to respond with love, joy, or peace.

In those moments, we must intentionally remind ourselves that we are branches extending from the Tree of Life. We should not let our physical response overshadow the spiritual strength and self-control God has deposited in us through the Holy Spirit. As we face difficult situations, let's remember that it's "not by might nor by power but by my Spirit" (Zechariah 4:6) says the Lord, that we overcome life's challenges. Today, rest in the confidence that we are branches created to bear fruit. We have been placed in this profession, or as a supporter, to continually be an extension of God's divine grace, peace, love, and joy, even in the most challenging circumstances.

Prayer:
Dear God,
Thank You for creating us with the ability to extend Your spiritual love in a physical form here on earth. As I work daily toward producing abundant, pleasing fruit, replace my natural responses of anger or harsh words with gentleness, stillness, quietness, and self-control. Let my actions reflect the grace and mercy You so freely give me, even when I don't deserve it.

Today, I receive Your Holy Spirit to guide and direct me as I choose the path of peace and compassion instead of chaos and strife. I choose to speak life and abundance, rather than death and lack. Guard my mind, heart, and words as I strive to be a fruitful branch that bears good fruit.

John 15:2 (NIV)
He cuts off every branch in me that bears no fruit, while every branch that does bear fruit, He prunes so that it will be even more fruitful.

Reflection and Prayer

Week of _____

Sunday:
_____
_____

Monday:
_____
_____

Tuesday:
_____
_____

Wednesday:
_____
_____

Thursday:
_____
_____

Friday:
_____
_____

Saturday:
_____
_____

	Sunday	Monday	Tuesday
3:00 - 4:00			
4:00 - 5:00			
5:00 - 6:00			
6:00 - 7:00			
7:00 - 8:00			
8:00 - 9:00			
9:00 - 10:00			
10:00 - 11:00			
11:00 - 12:00			
12:00 - 1:00			
1:00 - 2:00			
2:00 - 3:00			
3:00 - 4:00			
4:00 - 5:00			
5:00 - 6:00			
6:00 - 7:00			
7:00 - 8:00			

Wednesday	Thursday	Friday	Saturday

Week 24
Be a Beacon

There are times when the expectations, roles, and responsibilities of being an educator seem daunting and overwhelming. Some days, it feels like no one truly understands. Other days, it's like we are juggling caring for a family, striving for excellence in our professional duties, pursuing hobbies, and supporting spiritual or religious communities. If we choose to look at all of these tasks as burdens, they will continue to feel like daunting obstacles hanging over our heads, day after day.

When God designed and created the earth, He knew we would need others to help guide and support us during moments of uncertainty and despair. What is your outlook on supporting and helping others? Are you the one who constantly carries a half-empty glass? Are you a reliable friend or coworker, someone others can count on for grace and gentle motivation? Yes, life happens, but let us strive to encourage each other to reach the next goal. Sometimes, it's just a smile or a kind word that someone needs to shift the trajectory of their attitude or mindset during a difficult time.

As children of God, let's be intentional about setting the example of His grace, mercy, and love. Let us encourage our brothers and sisters to move forward toward fulfilling the rewarding assignment of finding hope in the hopeless, joy in sorrow, and peace in the storm.

Prayer:

Dear Lord,
I come to You with a grateful heart, thanking You that You did not create me to live in isolation. You provide a community of family, friends, believers, and coworkers to encourage me when it feels like my ankles are weighed down and moving forward seems impossible. Remind me that if I choose to encourage at least one person, that's one more person filled with hope, knowing that because of Your love, we can love each other through both the good and the difficult times.

Help me, Lord, to intentionally seek out the good in myself and others so that I can share the light You placed within me. I thank You that I am never alone, and I ask that You remove any selfish ways within me when it comes to being available to support others. Bless me with Your Spirit to be a beacon of hope and joy to someone who needs it today. Lord, if I am the one in need today, I know You are able to do the same for me. I receive Your hope, love, joy, peace, and comfort.

In Jesus' name, Amen!

Hebrews 10:24 (NIV)
And let us consider how we may spur one another on toward love and good deeds.

Reflection and Prayer

Week of _____

Sunday:

_____

_____

Monday:

_____

_____

Tuesday:

_____

_____

Wednesday:

_____

_____

Thursday:

_____

_____

Friday:

_____

_____

Saturday:

_____

_____

	Sunday	Monday	Tuesday
3:00 - 4:00			
4:00 - 5:00			
5:00 - 6:00			
6:00 - 7:00			
7:00 - 8:00			
8:00 - 9:00			
9:00 - 10:00			
10:00 - 11:00			
11:00 - 12:00			
12:00 - 1:00			
1:00 - 2:00			
2:00 - 3:00			
3:00 - 4:00			
4:00 - 5:00			
5:00 - 6:00			
6:00 - 7:00			
7:00 - 8:00			

Wednesday	Thursday	Friday	Saturday

Month of_____

SUNDAY	MONDAY	TUESDAY	WEDNESDAY

THURSDAY	FRIDAY	SATURDAY	NOTES

Week 25
Generous Wisdom

Day after day, we are asked to be creative, innovative, knowledgeable, flexible, passionate, loving, and sensitive, to name just a few. The to-do lists and character traits of an educator seem endless. Whether we are in the classroom, boardroom, front office, cafeteria, counselor's office, administrator's office, coach's office, or athletic area, the question often arises—how do we do it all? The answer is simple: God. His grace, mercy, wisdom, love, strength, and guidance allow us to go beyond our perceived and physical potential.

When we are unsure or lack wisdom on our next course of action, we can always turn to God. He generously grants wisdom, and we should approach Him boldly with our questions, fears, concerns, and praises. We can trust that God gives generously without holding our past mistakes against us. He is a God who wants us to succeed, and He is always there to provide support, comfort, and wisdom when we ask.

Prayer:

Dear God,
As I come to You once again, grant me the wisdom to make the best choices today and every day. Silence any thoughts that are not of You and ignite the flame that illuminates the path You want me to follow. I want to do what is right in Your eyes, Heavenly Father. Help me to excel in every area of my life. Grant me the wisdom and knowledge to understand and apply all that You are speaking into my life. I receive Your wisdom as the answer to my request.

In Jesus' name, Amen!

James 1:5 (KJV)
If any of you lacks wisdom, let him ask of God, who gives generously to all without reproach, and it will be given to him.

Reflection and Prayer

Week of _____

Sunday:
_____
_____

Monday:
_____
_____

Tuesday:
_____
_____

Wednesday:
_____
_____

Thursday:
_____
_____

Friday:
_____
_____

Saturday:
_____
_____

	Sunday	Monday	Tuesday
3:00 - 4:00			
4:00 - 5:00			
5:00 - 6:00			
6:00 - 7:00			
7:00 - 8:00			
8:00 - 9:00			
9:00 - 10:00			
10:00 - 11:00			
11:00 - 12:00			
12:00 - 1:00			
1:00 - 2:00			
2:00 - 3:00			
3:00 - 4:00			
4:00 - 5:00			
5:00 - 6:00			
6:00 - 7:00			
7:00 - 8:00			

Wednesday	Thursday	Friday	Saturday

Week 26
God's Hands

When God speaks, are we able to hear His voice? If the Lord was speaking to you, would you be able to recognize His voice? When a friend or loved one calls your name, how do you recognize his or her voice? As we spend time with friends or family members, the relationship and amount of time spent together determines how well we are able to recognize a particular voice. The more time we spend with someone, the easier it is to distinguish the voice in isolation or as a recognizable voice in a crowded room. Just as building physical relationships allow us to recognize familiar voices, spending time with the Lord gives us a greater inclination to hearing His voice. The more time that is spent praying, reading and sitting silently with God, the more able we are to hear His voice and follow as sheep follow the voice of the Shepherd. Ezekiel was called by God to go to Israel and speak His words to them. When the hand of the Lord is on our lives, He provides us with the necessary words to speak in the name of Jesus and deliver messages in the form of teaching, redirecting and counseling that is grounded in God's word and His directions. Let us be intentional about spending time with God and living with His hand on our lives as we work through the assignments He has put before us. Let us be living vessels who are willing to live and speak according to the words of the Lord. Whether it is found in the Bible or He speaks to us directly, let us be close enough to hear His voice and feel His hands!

Prayer:

Dear God,
As I navigate through life, some days it's easier to make time for You than others. Help me be intentional with my time—every minute, hour, and day—so that I can hear Your voice from the start of my day. Spending intentional time at the start of my day with You grounds me and prepares me for everything that comes my way. Keep Your loving eyes and hands on me as I seek to live as a light in all places. Bless, guide and redirect my path when necessary.

In Jesus' name, Amen!

Ezekiel 1:3 (NIV)
The word of the Lord came to Ezekiel the priest, the son of Buzi, by the Kebar River in the land of the Babylonians. There the hand of the Lord was upon him.

Reflection and Prayer

Week of _____

Sunday:
_____
_____

Monday:
_____
_____

Tuesday:
_____
_____

Wednesday:
_____
_____

Thursday:
_____
_____

Friday:
_____
_____

Saturday:
_____
_____

	Sunday	Monday	Tuesday
3:00 - 4:00			
4:00 - 5:00			
5:00 - 6:00			
6:00 - 7:00			
7:00 - 8:00			
8:00 - 9:00			
9:00 - 10:00			
10:00 - 11:00			
11:00 - 12:00			
12:00 - 1:00			
1:00 - 2:00			
2:00 - 3:00			
3:00 - 4:00			
4:00 - 5:00			
5:00 - 6:00			
6:00 - 7:00			
7:00 - 8:00			

Wednesday	Thursday	Friday	Saturday

Week 27
All is Well

As servants in God's kingdom, we are commanded to love one another. On most days, a simple compliment or a word of encouragement can be the small but powerful shift needed to change someone's mood or even the course of their day. However, we must also remember that we are not always on the receiving end of positive reinforcement, motivational words, or acknowledgment. There are times when we are assigned to be a motivator, offer our time, lend a listening ear, share a hug, smile, or remind someone that they are not alone. Just as John encouraged his friend Gaius with a heartfelt letter, we, too, are called to encourage a friend or colleague with authentic words, showing compassion and wishing them well in all areas of life.

Prayer:

Dear God,
As I go about my day, please open my eyes to see how I can encourage a friend, family member, student, or colleague who needs to hear a kind and uplifting word. Help me to be sensitive to the needs of others, regardless of my own circumstances. I pray that as I encourage others, Your joy and love will flow freely through me, and that I will intentionally seek to build someone up. Please heal and bless me physically, mentally, emotionally, spiritually, relationally and financially. Grant me prosperity in all areas and the resources to bless others. Thank You for using me today to uplift someone who may feel hopeless or helpless. Restore our faith, joy, and love.

In Jesus' name, Amen!

3 John 1:2 (KJV)

Beloved, I wish above all things that thou mayest prosper and be in health, even as thy soul prospereth.

Reflection and Prayer

Week of _____

Sunday:

_____

_____

Monday:

_____

_____

Tuesday:

_____

_____

Wednesday:

_____

_____

Thursday:

_____

_____

Friday:

_____

_____

Saturday:

_____

_____

	Sunday	Monday	Tuesday
3:00 - 4:00			
4:00 - 5:00			
5:00 - 6:00			
6:00 - 7:00			
7:00 - 8:00			
8:00 - 9:00			
9:00 - 10:00			
10:00 - 11:00			
11:00 - 12:00			
12:00 - 1:00			
1:00 - 2:00			
2:00 - 3:00			
3:00 - 4:00			
4:00 - 5:00			
5:00 - 6:00			
6:00 - 7:00			
7:00 - 8:00			

Wednesday	Thursday	Friday	Saturday

Week 28

Devoted Prayers

In many educational environments, mentioning God or public prayer is not allowed. However, prayer becomes acceptable and welcomed in response to tragedy. When a crisis strikes, we are encouraged to pray for one another or pause for a moment of silence. Why should we be reactive in prayer rather than proactive? We should develop a habit of praying throughout the day. We can start our day with prayers for protection, guidance, and wisdom for our friends, family, sphere of influence, students, district, church, community and nation, to name a few. Our midday prayers can be grounded in love while continued strength, love, and discernment are petitioned. As we prepare to close our day, gratitude can flow from our hearts for the day's blessings.

Let us shift our posture from reactive prayer to proactive prayer. At the start of our day, let us intentionally set aside time to meet with God, offering thanks, praise, and petitions. Throughout the day, we can pray for wisdom, strength, and guidance. Even if we cannot pray openly as a class or in our educational community, we can still pray in our homes, in our cars, silently as we walk through the halls, quietly in our classrooms, before making decisions in the boardroom, and before leading others in any capacity. As we move forward, let's be intentional about creating or finding a community of believers who can pray for the positive changes we hope to see in our classrooms, schools, districts, boardrooms, and communities.

Prayer:

Dear God,
I thank You for this day and the opportunity to bring my petitions before You. First, I want to thank You for the many blessings You have showered upon me, my family, friends, school, and community. While everything may not be perfect, I choose to focus on the positive and hope for brighter days. The very ability to read or listen to this prayer is a blessing in itself. Lord, help me to be a change agent as I encourage my students, coworkers, family members and friends. Grant me the strength to pray powerful and bold prayers in the face of challenging situations. Remind me to remain devoted to proactive prayers, believing in faith for the positive and continuous changes that are possible in our schools, community, and nation. I give You thanks in advance for my answered prayers.

In Jesus' name. Amen!

Colossians 4:2 (NIV)

Devote yourselves to prayer, being watchful and thankful.

Reflection and Prayer

Week of _____

Sunday:

_____

_____

Monday:

_____

_____

Tuesday:

_____

_____

Wednesday:

_____

_____

Thursday:

_____

_____

Friday:

_____

_____

Saturday:

_____

_____

	Sunday	Monday	Tuesday
3:00 - 4:00			
4:00 - 5:00			
5:00 - 6:00			
6:00 - 7:00			
7:00 - 8:00			
8:00 - 9:00			
9:00 - 10:00			
10:00 - 11:00			
11:00 - 12:00			
12:00 - 1:00			
1:00 - 2:00			
2:00 - 3:00			
3:00 - 4:00			
4:00 - 5:00			
5:00 - 6:00			
6:00 - 7:00			
7:00 - 8:00			

Wednesday	Thursday	Friday	Saturday

Month of_____

SUNDAY	MONDAY	TUESDAY	WEDNESDAY

THURSDAY	FRIDAY	SATURDAY	NOTES

Week 29

Darkness to Light

As children, many of us can recall being afraid of the dark. Our imagination would create images, often accompanied by sounds, that rarely reflected reality. A tree limb brushing against the window would become the star of a full-length movie, complete with special effects. The damp towel hanging on the closet door would transform into the ghost we saw in that movie we were told not to watch. Isn't it amazing how powerful our minds can be? Just as false images were created in our childhood, the enemy attempts to do the same by using false images and scenarios to cloud the reality of the promises God has for us as His chosen people.

When we are immobilized by fear, we are unable to accomplish the assignments that God has beautifully planned for us. As educators, we carefully plan lessons designed to captivate our students' attention, guiding them through the content they are expected to learn and apply. Likewise, God prepares lessons for us, pulling us out of darkness and guiding us toward His light. He provides knowledge and direction through a relationship with Him and His Word, which we are expected to apply in our lives.

Today, be reminded that we are chosen by God to live in the light and be a light to others. We are no longer in darkness. Just as a child feels relief when the sun shines through at daybreak, we should also find comfort knowing that God's Son paid the ultimate price, taking us out of darkness and offering us the gift of eternal life and light.

Prayer:

Dear God,
Thank You for sending Your only Son, Jesus Christ, to die on the cross to save me from my sins. Remind me in those dark times when I am fearful that I have eternal life and light in You. Today, I am grateful that You chose me, and I will praise Your name forever.

1 Peter 2:9 (KJV)

But you are a chosen people, a royal priesthood, a holy nation, God's special possession, that you may declare the praises of Him who called you out of darkness into His wonderful light.

Reflection and Prayer

Week of _____

Sunday:

_____

_____

Monday:

_____

_____

Tuesday:

_____

_____

Wednesday:

_____

_____

Thursday:

_____

_____

Friday:

_____

_____

Saturday:

_____

_____

	Sunday	Monday	Tuesday
3:00 - 4:00			
4:00 - 5:00			
5:00 - 6:00			
6:00 - 7:00			
7:00 - 8:00			
8:00 - 9:00			
9:00 - 10:00			
10:00 - 11:00			
11:00 - 12:00			
12:00 - 1:00			
1:00 - 2:00			
2:00 - 3:00			
3:00 - 4:00			
4:00 - 5:00			
5:00 - 6:00			
6:00 - 7:00			
7:00 - 8:00			

Wednesday	Thursday	Friday	Saturday

Week 30
Your Grace is Sufficient

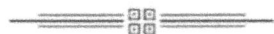

Some days are just tough, and even the best plans and intentions may not lead to success. It's in those moments that we must remember God's grace is sufficient to carry us from task to task and from glory to glory.

Prayer:

Dear God,

I ask You today, to heal my heart and redirect my plans according to Your will. Please comfort me in the midst of my perceived failures. I know that You are already working behind the scenes to fix what I see as mistakes, and I graciously accept Your new direction.

Give me peace and strengthen my faith as I pivot according to Your plans. Help me to love myself the way You love me and to give myself the grace to be perfectly imperfect. I believe in You and in Your direction for both my day and my life. I surrender it all to You, knowing that I am receiving Your power in my weakness.

I receive everything You have spoken over my life as I move forward in Your strength. Your grace is sufficient for me, and I trust in You. In Jesus' mighty name, Amen.

2 Corinthians 12:9 (NIV)
But He said to me, "My grace is sufficient for you, for my power is made perfect in weakness." Therefore, I will boast all the more gladly about my weaknesses, so that Christ's power may rest on me.

Reflection and Prayer

Week of _____

Sunday:

_____

_____

Monday:

_____

_____

Tuesday:

_____

_____

Wednesday:

_____

_____

Thursday:

_____

_____

Friday:

_____

_____

Saturday:

_____

_____

	Sunday	Monday	Tuesday
3:00 - 4:00			
4:00 - 5:00			
5:00 - 6:00			
6:00 - 7:00			
7:00 - 8:00			
8:00 - 9:00			
9:00 - 10:00			
10:00 - 11:00			
11:00 - 12:00			
12:00 - 1:00			
1:00 - 2:00			
2:00 - 3:00			
3:00 - 4:00			
4:00 - 5:00			
5:00 - 6:00			
6:00 - 7:00			
7:00 - 8:00			

Wednesday	Thursday	Friday	Saturday

Week 31
Do Not Be Anxious

It's early in the morning. Our hearts are racing and we can't quiet our minds because we know what awaits us. The never-ending "to-do" list occupies the moments that should be dedicated to rest and rejuvenation. In these unsettling times, God is inviting us to come to Him and embrace this moment He has set aside just for time with Him. Replace the uneasiness of this moment with prayer. Allow God's presence to fill the atmosphere and meditate on His goodness as He directs this time together.

Prayer:

Dear God,

As this day begins, You know the thoughts, emotions, and concerns that have greeted me at an early hour. You are meeting with me right now, as I offer the first moments of my day to You. As the hours and minutes move closer to the start of my day, I ask that You meet me here and settle my mind with Your peace as I meditate on Your sweet and gentle spirit.

As it is written in Your word, I command the spirit of anxiety to leave, and I step forward in prayer with thanksgiving. I am thankful for Your gift of peace, as You guard my heart and mind. I release my concerns to You, and I accept the freedom You give by supplying all of my needs. I am grateful for all that You have provided and will provide as I move forward with confidence, knowing that You are Jehovah Jireh, my Provider.

Thank You for meeting me during this moment to refresh my mind, heart, body, and spirit as I prepare for another day. With a grateful heart, I receive Your love and peace.

In Jesus' name. Amen.

Philippians 4:6-7 (NIV)

Do not be anxious about anything, but in every situation, by prayer and petition, with thanksgiving, present your requests to God. And the peace of God, which transcends all understanding, will guard your hearts and your minds in Christ Jesus.

Reflection and Prayer

Week of _____

Sunday:
_____
_____

Monday:
_____
_____

Tuesday:
_____
_____

Wednesday:
_____
_____

Thursday:
_____
_____

Friday:
_____
_____

Saturday:
_____
_____

	Sunday	Monday	Tuesday
3:00 - 4:00			
4:00 - 5:00			
5:00 - 6:00			
6:00 - 7:00			
7:00 - 8:00			
8:00 - 9:00			
9:00 - 10:00			
10:00 - 11:00			
11:00 - 12:00			
12:00 - 1:00			
1:00 - 2:00			
2:00 - 3:00			
3:00 - 4:00			
4:00 - 5:00			
5:00 - 6:00			
6:00 - 7:00			
7:00 - 8:00			

Wednesday	Thursday	Friday	Saturday

Week 32
Rest For the Weary

I've heard it more times than I can count: "Educators aren't in it for the money." But is that really true? If we're not in it for the money, what are we in it for? The answer may vary from person to person, just as the needs we bring to God vary. The juggling of academic, behavioral, mental, economic, personal, and social demands forces us to gently balance the roles of educator and caregiver during our prescribed hours. Then, we shift gears, to tackle the lists that extend well beyond the end of the day, striving to get just about everything done. At times, the burdens can feel unbearable. But as we bring our needs to God, Holy Spirit reminds us that our Heavenly Father provides a safe place to lay down our burdens, so we can rest and be renewed to give our best.

Prayer:

Heavenly Father,

I come to You right now, asking for the strength I need to make it through today. I am not seeking to merely make it through the day, but I am committed to thriving as I pour into the students and individuals You have entrusted to me. I accept the charge to lead, support, encourage, uplift, educate, and guide everyone in my sphere of influence.

You know when I am mentally, physically, spiritually, or emotionally tired. I accept Your invitation to come to You when I am weary and burdened, to find a place of sweet rest. At this moment, I lay my burdens at Your feet, and I am energized by Your Spirit that lives within me. The rest You provide gives me the strength to walk confidently through this day, knowing that I have a loving Father who is always willing to carry my burdens so that I can fulfill His purpose for my life.

I thank You for the gift of rest.

In Jesus' mighty name. Amen!

Matthew 11:28 (KJV)
Come to me, all you who are weary and burdened, and I will give you rest.

Reflection and Prayer

Week of _____

Sunday:

_____

_____

Monday:

_____

_____

Tuesday:

_____

_____

Wednesday:

_____

_____

Thursday:

_____

_____

Friday:

_____

_____

Saturday:

_____

_____

	Sunday	Monday	Tuesday
3:00 - 4:00			
4:00 - 5:00			
5:00 - 6:00			
6:00 - 7:00			
7:00 - 8:00			
8:00 - 9:00			
9:00 - 10:00			
10:00 - 11:00			
11:00 - 12:00			
12:00 - 1:00			
1:00 - 2:00			
2:00 - 3:00			
3:00 - 4:00			
4:00 - 5:00			
5:00 - 6:00			
6:00 - 7:00			
7:00 - 8:00			

Wednesday	Thursday	Friday	Saturday

Month of_____

SUNDAY	MONDAY	TUESDAY	WEDNESDAY

THURSDAY	FRIDAY	SATURDAY	NOTES

Week 33
Healing Waters

As Moses led the Israelites from the Red Sea into the Desert of Shur, they grumbled and complained, because they were weary and thirsty, with no water in sight. Moses cried out to the Lord, and He answered by providing more than they had asked for. He gave them water to quench their thirst and palm trees for shade and rest. Just like the Israelites, there are times when life becomes overwhelming, and we feel as though we are traveling with no end in sight. We are tired of the daily struggles and thirsty for what we believe will lead to a more peaceful and fulfilling life. God reminds us that if we call on Him, He will provide water and shade during the periods in our lives that feel like a desert, dry and void of life. Though these times may seem like there is no life or growth, we should not be disheartened. We must stay committed to the assignment God has given us and He will bless us with more than we asked for. He will provide healing water to refresh our body, mind, and spirit, to complete the journey set before us.

Prayer:

Dear God, Mighty Jehovah Rapha,

I thank You for being our God who heals. On this day, I am grateful for Your healing waters that refresh, heal, and satisfy our bodies. As I experience different seasons of drought in various areas of my life, I am thankful for Your reminder that these seasons are temporary and if I call on Your mighty name, You will provide me with shade under Your mighty palm trees and healing waters that never run dry.

In Jesus's name, Amen.

Exodus 15:26 (KJV)

Then they came to Elim, where there were twelve springs and seventy palm trees, and they camped there near the water.

Reflection and Prayer

Week of _____

Sunday:

_____

_____

Monday:

_____

_____

Tuesday:

_____

_____

Wednesday:

_____

_____

Thursday:

_____

_____

Friday:

_____

_____

Saturday:

_____

_____

	Sunday	Monday	Tuesday
3:00 - 4:00			
4:00 - 5:00			
5:00 - 6:00			
6:00 - 7:00			
7:00 - 8:00			
8:00 - 9:00			
9:00 - 10:00			
10:00 - 11:00			
11:00 - 12:00			
12:00 - 1:00			
1:00 - 2:00			
2:00 - 3:00			
3:00 - 4:00			
4:00 - 5:00			
5:00 - 6:00			
6:00 - 7:00			
7:00 - 8:00			

Wednesday	Thursday	Friday	Saturday

Week 34

Feed My Sheep

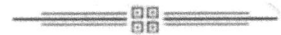

The unfortunate truth is that some educators enter classrooms with students who have been subjected to less-than-favorable lives. Their clothes are dirty, their hair isn't combed, their teeth weren't brushed, they didn't get enough sleep, and they lack the basic necessities to be fully prepared for the day. Are these children to blame for their unfortunate circumstances? What about a child who struggles due to genetics or an undiagnosed disability? Should that child receive less education or love due to circumstances beyond his or her control?

Before Jesus fed the five thousand, He saw their need for guidance. He referred to them as sheep without a shepherd, and His compassion led Him to teach and feed them. As we receive students, parents, and community members who need guidance, we should not berate or speak ill of them to others. Though it can be difficult, we are called to show the same love and compassion that Jesus demonstrated. As we follow His example, we learn that Jesus did not meet only academic or spiritual needs. He also provided the physical need for food, which highlights His understanding of the holistic needs of those He served. As we serve in various capacities, we should ask for knowledge and awareness to be in tune and available to meet the needs of the whole child.

Prayer:

Dear God,
As we begin this day, please open my heart to be sensitive to the needs of those around me. Help me to show compassion without judgment toward individuals or families who lack basic necessities. Grant me the wisdom to speak kindly when needed and provide support—whether academically, socially, behaviorally or nutritionally. This profession is a calling, and as Your chosen vessel, remind me that I am here to serve in a greater capacity in Your kingdom. I am grateful for all that You have blessed me with, and I pray that You will provide for those who are struggling, homeless, or hungry in my school, district, community, and nation. Bless us, Lord.

In Jesus' name, Amen!

Mark 6:34

When Jesus landed and saw a large crowd, He had compassion on them, because they were like sheep without a shepherd. So He began teaching them many things.

Reflection and Prayer

Week of _____

Sunday:

_____

_____

Monday:

_____

_____

Tuesday:

_____

_____

Wednesday:

_____

_____

Thursday:

_____

_____

Friday:

_____

_____

Saturday:

_____

_____

	Sunday	Monday	Tuesday
3:00 - 4:00			
4:00 - 5:00			
5:00 - 6:00			
6:00 - 7:00			
7:00 - 8:00			
8:00 - 9:00			
9:00 - 10:00			
10:00 - 11:00			
11:00 - 12:00			
12:00 - 1:00			
1:00 - 2:00			
2:00 - 3:00			
3:00 - 4:00			
4:00 - 5:00			
5:00 - 6:00			
6:00 - 7:00			
7:00 - 8:00			

Wednesday	Thursday	Friday	Saturday

Week 35
<u>Lacking Nothing</u>

God's provision and love cannot be measured solely in tangible assets. Yes, we are children of the King, and He wants us to have His best, but receiving His abundance comes from the immeasurable wealth found in a personal relationship with Him. Just for a moment, think about the number of individuals who have abundant earthly wealth but struggle to live in peace. Their constant need to attain or achieve more surpasses their contentment with their current blessings.

Someone might say, "How can I be content when my debt exceeds my income or I'm struggling with health issues?" The physical reality of any given situation can blur the assurance that our Heavenly Father is our shepherd and that He is able to provide for all our needs. This provision isn't based on superficial desires but on the understanding that the best provision is knowing that we have direct access to God, where we can present our requests with the confidence that He hears us.

In this moment, think about some of the ways God has provided or answered prayers. If you are experiencing lack in any area, take a moment to present your requests to God and read the entire chapter of Psalm 23. Then, take a few minutes to write and speak what you are believing for in the present tense, with God's promise that He is our Shepherd and we lack nothing. Let's practice attaching God's word to what we are believing for, writing and speaking it boldly until God answers. God has the provision, but He is also expecting us to start the process of movement to make room for Him to complete what He has already planned for us.

Let us speak and believe that we lack nothing, and be prepared for God to show up and show out in our lives!

Prayer:

Dear God, my Shepherd,
I thank You that I lack nothing. I am eternally grateful that my relationship with You provides access to healing, peace, wealth, joy, grace, mercy, and forgiveness. In this moment, I bring my heart's desires to You. I ask that You incline Your ear to my words and bless me according to the word of God in Psalm 23, that states I lack nothing. I ask and receive Your provision in every area of my life. As You bless me, I will be faithful in giving my monetary and non-monetary tithe, such as my time. Bless those in need. Heal those who are hurting, and help me to share my testimony about Your goodness to those who are struggling to believe. You are my Shepherd, and I lack nothing. I will walk boldly from this day forward, believing, speaking, and writing it with the assurance that Your words will not return void. Thank You for today's blessings.

In Jesus' name, Amen!

Psalm 23:1 (NIV)
The Lord is my shepherd; I lack nothing.

Reflection and Prayer

Week of _____

Sunday:
_____
_____

Monday:
_____
_____

Tuesday:
_____
_____

Wednesday:
_____
_____

Thursday:
_____
_____

Friday:
_____
_____

Saturday:
_____
_____

	Sunday	Monday	Tuesday
3:00 - 4:00			
4:00 - 5:00			
5:00 - 6:00			
6:00 - 7:00			
7:00 - 8:00			
8:00 - 9:00			
9:00 - 10:00			
10:00 - 11:00			
11:00 - 12:00			
12:00 - 1:00			
1:00 - 2:00			
2:00 - 3:00			
3:00 - 4:00			
4:00 - 5:00			
5:00 - 6:00			
6:00 - 7:00			
7:00 - 8:00			

Wednesday	Thursday	Friday	Saturday

Week 36
The Greatest Commandments

During our quiet time with our Heavenly Father, we should seek to hear from Him and act upon His directions. As you sit quietly today, invite the Holy Spirit to fill your senses with the sweet aroma of the Lord. Ask the Lord to let your heart overflow with love for Him and others. Just as Jesus instructed the Pharisees on the two greatest commandments, let's strive daily to love the Lord our God with our whole heart and love our neighbor as ourselves. Loving might look like choosing to be silent when you have every right to clear your name or prove your point. It might look like choosing to show compassion to a child or adult who is having a difficult day or week. It might be sitting quietly with a friend who is struggling to see the value of remaining committed in a challenging situation. It might look like volunteering within the community and allowing someone else's light to shine brightly. Or it might look like what appears to be the most difficult, loving someone who seems unlovable. Let's pray that as we build our relationship with the Lord, we will always be reminded of the two greatest commandments: Love the Lord your God with all your heart and love your neighbor as yourself. As your prayer life grows deeper and your relationship with God flourishes, always remember that God has a perfect plan for every assignment. Pray bold prayers and continuously speak every word God has promised over your life. As you love God and others, don't forget to love yourself!! YOU ARE CHOSEN!!

Prayer:

Dear God,
I thank You for this day. I am so grateful that You sent Your Son, Jesus, to die on the cross to save me from my sins. I believe and confess that You are Lord and Savior over my life. Please forgive me for anything that I have done that has not been pleasing in Your sight. I ask for Your forgiveness if I have intentionally or unintentionally offended someone, especially a child or person in my care or sphere of influence. Quiet my mind and heart today so that I can clearly hear from You. Be my peace during the storm and my banner that flies high as I praise and glorify Your name. I ask that you show me how to love with Your love today. I thank You for filling my heart with love that overflows for you and others.

In Jesus' mighty name – AMEN!

Matthew 22:37-38 (NIV)

Jesus replied: "'Love the Lord your God with all your heart and with all your soul and with all your mind. This is the first and greatest commandment. And the second is like it: 'Love your neighbor as yourself.

Reflection and Prayer

Week of _____

Sunday:
_____
_____

Monday:
_____
_____

Tuesday:
_____
_____

Wednesday:
_____
_____

Thursday:
_____
_____

Friday:
_____
_____

Saturday:
_____
_____

	Sunday	Monday	Tuesday
3:00 - 4:00			
4:00 - 5:00			
5:00 - 6:00			
6:00 - 7:00			
7:00 - 8:00			
8:00 - 9:00			
9:00 - 10:00			
10:00 - 11:00			
11:00 - 12:00			
12:00 - 1:00			
1:00 - 2:00			
2:00 - 3:00			
3:00 - 4:00			
4:00 - 5:00			
5:00 - 6:00			
6:00 - 7:00			
7:00 - 8:00			

Wednesday	Thursday	Friday	Saturday

Reflection and Prayer

Week of _____

Reflection and Prayer

Week of _____

Reflection and Prayer

Week of _____

Reflection and Prayer

Week of _____

Reflection and Prayer

Week of _____

Reflection and Prayer

Week of _____

Reflection and Prayer

Week of _____

Reflection and Prayer

Week of _____

Reflection and Prayer

Week of _____

Reflection and Prayer

Week of _____

Reflection and Prayer

Week of _____

Reflection and Prayer

Week of _____

Reflection and Prayer

Week of _____

Reflection and Prayer

Week of _____

Reflection and Prayer

Week of _____

Reflection and Prayer

Week of _____

Reflection and Prayer

Week of _____

Reflection and Prayer

Week of _____

Reflection and Prayer

Week of _____

Reflection and Prayer

Week of _____

Reflection and Prayer

Week of _____

Reflection and Prayer

Week of _____

Reflection and Prayer

Week of _____

Reflection and Prayer

Week of _____

Reflection and Prayer

Week of _____

Reflection and Prayer

Week of _____

Reflection and Prayer

Week of _____

Reflection and Prayer

Week of _____

Reflection and Prayer

Week of _____

Reflection and Prayer

Week of _____

Reflection and Prayer

Week of _____

Reflection and Prayer

Week of _____

Reflection and Prayer

Week of _____

Reflection and Prayer

Week of _____

Reflection and Prayer

Week of _____

Reflection and Prayer

Week of _____

Reflection and Prayer

Week of _____

Reflection and Prayer

Week of _____

Reflection and Prayer

Week of _____

Reflection and Prayer

Week of _____